Charles Williams Chancellor, Maryland State Board of Health

The Sanitation of Cities and Towns and the Agricultural Utilization

of Excretal Matters

Report on improved methods of sewage disposal and water supplies

Charles Williams Chancellor, Maryland State Board of Health

The Sanitation of Cities and Towns and the Agricultural Utilization of Excretal Matters
Report on improved methods of sewage disposal and water supplies

ISBN/EAN: 9783337735487

Printed in Europe, USA, Canada, Australia, Japan

Cover: Foto ©Andreas Hilbeck / pixelio.de

More available books at **www.hansebooks.com**

MARYLAND
STATE BOARD OF HEALTH.
1887.

THE SANITATION OF CITIES AND TOWNS
AND THE
AGRICULTURAL UTILIZATION OF EXCRETAL MATTERS.

REPORT
ON
Improved Methods of Sewage Disposal
AND
Water Supplies.

BY

C. W. CHANCELLOR, M. D.,

Secretary of the State Board of Health of Maryland ; Member of the American
Public Health Association ; Fellow of the Society of Science, Letters
and Art, London, &c., &c.

BALTIMORE:
THE SUN BOOK AND JOB PRINTING OFFICE.
1887.

INTRODUCTORY LETTER.

To His Excellency Henry Lloyd,

Governor of Maryland:

Dear Sir—In pursuance of a resolution passed by the State Board of Health on the 19th day of November, 1886, and approved by your Excellency, authorizing me to proceed to Europe to investigate the most recent plans in practical operation for the disposal and utilization of household sewage, especially with reference to the sanitation of Maryland towns, and to report thereon, I herewith present the result of my labors.

Undertaking the investigation with no preconceived notions of my own as to how the problem was to be solved; determined not to be influenced by appeals in favor of any particular scheme, however highly recommended; anxious to receive testimony from all parties, to hear all that could be said and to see all that could be seen, I have been guided not only by a fairly intimate acquaintance with what has been made public during the last ten or fifteen years on the "vexed question" of town sewerage, but by such experience as could be derived from a personal examination of the principal systems in operation in England, France, Germany, Belgium, and Holland.

My views on some points, I am well aware, will not be endorsed by certain sanitarians and engineers in this country, but my conclusions have been formed on what I consider a sound "basis of facts," and, I must believe, a practical working out of the details will show them to be correct.

The principal difficulties which have hitherto environed the subject seem to have arisen from a determination to carry out "foregone conclusions," overlooking the important facts that no one system is universally applicable, and that what may do for one town will not do for another under totally different circumstances.

How then are communities to get out of the difficulties in which they are placed? There is a gleam of hope in a direction only recently pointed out, and this is by the adoption of a modification of existing pneumatic systems, such as is described in Chapter XXIV of this report, for large centres of population. And for smaller cities and towns, not able to sustain expenditures proportionate to those of large and wealthy communities; for public institutions, manufactories, private residences, &c., by the use of a very recent invention, described in the Appendix to this report, the main features of which will be gathered from its name, "The Separating and Filtrating Process for Household Sewage." I have carefully studied these devices and can confidently recommend their adoption.

Very Respectfully, Yours,

C. W. CHANCELLOR, M. D.,
Secretary and Executive Officer,
Maryland State Board of Health.

BALTIMORE, May 17th, 1887.

Contents.

Sewage Disposal and Water Supplies.

CHAPTER I

THE QUESTION OF SEWAGE DISPOSAL.

THE whole question of the disposal of town sewage is manifestly one of the greatest difficulty as well as of the greatest importance. Sewage, if left to remain in or near the neighborhood of dwellings or occupied houses, is alike destructive to health and comfort, and if there is anything in the teachings of sanitary science it is an imperative duty of all corporations to get rid of the nuisance at whatever cost. If, in getting rid of the nuisance from a sanitary standpoint, anything is to be made of it from an agricultural point of view, good and well, let it be done. But, in taking a commercial view of the question, it is to be remembered that our farmers are intelligent men, and will not use the material unless it is worth using.

In connection with the supply of manure to agricultural districts, it may be taken as a maxim that the more concentrated it is, the cheaper it will be to the farmer. The transportation of a cheap manure is obviously the same as that of a dear manure, and the tendency is now, very properly, to increase the value in a given quantity of manure. If it is worth fifty dollars per ton, so much the better, provided it contains the same value as could be supplied by fifty dollars' worth of an inferior manure at five dollars per ton.

It is now agreed, that sewage matter of towns, even when largely diluted with water, is a fertilizer of some value. and the point to be settled is whether it can be conveyed to the land at a cost which will render it pecuniarily valuable to the farmer.

On this point Mr. Scott Burn remarks: "If the present "system of tubular house drains, leading to sewers, and these "again to streams and rivers, is to be carried out, then it is "clear that on the one hand we commit a great waste in an "agricultural point of view, by throwing needlessly away that "which, beyond all doubt, contains a comparatively large quan- "tity of fertilizing materials useful for certain crops: and on "the other, we commit a great wrong in a social and sanitary "point of view, by polluting our streams and rivers. poisoning "the very sources from which we obtain the water useful for "household purposes, or making our rivers huge open cesspools, "to flow past or through our towns, sending forth from day "to day the seeds of death and disease."

But even supposing that the present water-carriage method of conveying our town sewage to river outfalls is discontinued. and plans adopted by which the liquid sewage is prevented from entering the river, and dealt with either by pumping it directly on the land, or treated so as to make it part with its fertilizing matter in a solid form, still the present system of drains, necessitating as it does the use of water to make them efficient, presents difficulties which seem inherent in the system: for it is evident the more the population becomes extended, and the farther the present principles—the conveying through the drains "all the refuse which can be estimated to float in water"—are carried out, the greater the quantity of water required, and the greater the decrease in the value of the sewage liquid obtained.

In view of these points, attention has been directed to devising some plan by which both the agricultural and sanitary requirements of the question can be met. Some—and the number is fast increasing—go further and affirm that water-carriage is in principle wrong ; that no modification of the practice founded on it will meet the difficulty ; that we shall have to begin again—inaugurate another system—at least so far as the excretal result of our population is concerned.

CHAPTER II.

GENERAL PRINCIPLES TO BE OBSERVED.

THE following may be considered as the general principles upon which the sewerage of towns is to be based :

1. That the proper sewering of a large town depends in a measure on an adequate and regulated supply of water for domestic uses.

2. That two outfalls, independent of each other, should be provided, one for the discharge of the natural or surface waters, and the other for the discharge of the excretal and household sewage.

3. That in order to perfectly drain the surface and sub-soil of a town. so as to free it from dampness, and carry off as quickly as possible the natural waters, where the conditions of

the surface are not such as to accomplish the object without artificial means being provided, a system of permeable drains or sewers should be constructed to receive the surface waters and washings which may be discharged into natural water-courses not used for domestic purposes.

4. That in towns where the surface drainage is good and where outfalls are already provided, by streams or rivers, for the discharge of the natural waters, it is only necessary to make provision for the drainage of the low-lying areas, and to provide separate pipes and outfalls for the excretal and household matters, which should be conveyed as fast as produced to an outlying depot or central station at a convenient and unobjectionable place quite clear of the town.

5. That no correct general views of sewerage can prevail while we continue to regard a stream or river as the natural or suitable trunk sewer for excretal and household wastes, which, according to the state of the river, are spread upon its banks to contaminate the air, or are duly infused into its waters to be afterwards exposed to the same vicious effects and to destroy whatever of life may exist within the water.

6. That, in order to carry off excretal and household wastes without contaminating the atmosphere of the town by the escape of effluvia through the numerous inlets which are necessary for surface drainage, a system of impermeable pipes should be provided, distinct from the permeable drains or sewers, to discharge without intermission and at short intervals into an outfall independent of any river or stream, except for a practically pure effluent.

7. That at the outlet for excretal and household sewage a depot or station should be formed, and works established for converting the sewage matters into an agent or "poudrette" suitable for agricultural and horticultural purposes.

8. That in all towns where an improper system of sewerage works have already been executed, practical operations for a proper system become more difficult, especially if we have to reconcile these with the improved details which correct principles would induce us to prefer.

9. That the saturation of the soil in or near a town by crude sewage matters is a constant concomitant of epidemic diseases, while a proportionate exemption from such maladies has followed the removal of this source of aerial pollution.

10. That the sole purpose of sewers, as distinguished from the drains of a town, should be that of affording a passage for the conveyance of excrementitious matters and household wastes only, all manufactories and trades being required to clean their own waste; not of course to convert it into pure water, but to deprive it of its power to become a nuisance to others when discharged into the public drains or elsewhere.

11. That the conveyance of sewage should be immediate and thorough, every particle committed to the entire ramification of pipes being kept in ceaseless motion until it arrives at the final collecting place; and this desideratum can only be attained in one of three ways: (1) By great declivity of the sewer; (2) By the artificial force of water; (3) By pneumatic pressure or suction, to drive or draw forward the matter.

12. That without one or other of these aids sewers, especially large sewers during dry seasons, will become elongated reservoirs or cesspools in which the refuse matters remain decomposing for days and weeks, sending up the most pernicious gases into the drains and water-closets of houses, and, in the case of large drains, through the ventilating apertures and manholes into the streets of the town.

13. That artificial scouring or flushing of sewers may be regarded as an expensive and troublesome correction of some of the evils occasioned by deficient declivity, and one some-

times attended with mischievous consequences, viz : the forcing up of the sewage into the streets from some of the lower sewers, which become surcharged with flushing water during the process ; and furthermore that flushing is inapplicable to any method which proposes to preserve the sewage for agricultural uses.

14. That during the putrefaction of excretal sewage and household wastes, which takes place within from 24 to 48 hours after their discharge, the nitrogen they contain, and which is one of their most useful constituents, is converted into ammonia, which is disengaged, and if this process should take place in the open air, it mingles with the atmosphere in the form of carbonate of ammonia, and leaves the sewage in a much less valuable condition for fertilizing purposes.

15. That the gases engendered by the putrefying matters of sewage, and which too often bring pestilence and death to our homes, would, if retained in the sewage, constitute its most valuable fertilizing properties, and that we should, in order to protect the public health, as well as to convert the fructifying matters into a valuable manure, adopt the best practicable methods of applying the purifying process before these dangerous properties have been developed.

16. That chemistry supplies us with the means by which the most offensive and deleterious properties of the sewage may be suppressed and its useful properties safely retained, and there is no reason why a tank or receptacle in which sewage is collected and stored at the outfall, should be, if properly arranged, in any respect disgusting to the senses or injurious to the health of human beings.

17. That it appears probable such an operation will generally pay its own expenses ; but as some such measure is absolutely necessary for the protection of the public health in all centres of population, even though involving expense, it should be the

duty of municipal authorities to carry it out, just as much as arrangements devolving upon them for the removal of street dirt or any other refuse from the town.

18. That the sewage cleared of its solid matter by deodorising and precipitating agents may be used anywhere, and any quantity of it applied to the land without risk of injury to health and without creating as much offensiveness as is experienced from farm-yard and other solid manures applied as top dressings.

19. That the liquid portion of the sewage thus cleared of its solid matters, though pure enough to be emptied into watercourses not appropriated to domestic uses, will still retain considerable value as a manure and may be applied with benefit to the neighboring lands in any reasonable quantity; but that all land upon which it is applied, if not naturally porous, should be artificially drained, since the liquid, if allowed to stagnate in large quantities on the surface, would, as in common irrigation, be likely to engender disease among the neighboring inhabitants, or in cattle exposed to its influence.

20. That public health and economy are the cardinal objects which should be distinctly kept in view in the design and execution of any sewerage system and that these two objects are more certainly and effectually attained when the sewage is carried by pneumatic pressure or suction, for by this means the matter may be collected and dispersed without any detriment to health, and its removal effected at such cost as will be, at least, balanced by converting it readily into a portable manure, whereas, by any plan of water-carriage yet devised, it is rendered quite valueless as a fertilizing agent by the immense dilution necessary, and eventually pollutes water or soil, as it falls into streams or flows upon the surface of the earth.

21. That the cost of a pneumatic system may be reduced to a minimum by skillful arrangements, which seem to have

been attained in the Le Marquand system ; but our experience is yet insufficient to enable us to determine this question with that precision which further knowledge will secure, or to estimate *all* the advantages with the exactness necessary for forming a just comparison between the proposed and the present methods. It is quite certain, however, that excrementitious and other household waste matters are far too valuable to be thrown away, and that the question of their conservation and appropriation depends upon the possibilities of an efficient pneumatic system.

22. That as an essential part of any general system of sewerage conducive to the health of the entire population, the connection of every house with the sewers should be commanded and enforced by public authority and carried into immediate effect without favor or evasion ; and especially in the construction of all new buildings should this connection be regarded as imperative general orders, sanctioned by the public well-being, and, if necessary, to be obeyed under official superintendence.

Formerly when a town was to be sewered the one question of river or no river was the grand determinal one for the disposal of refuse matters ; how to get rid of the animal ordure and kitchen slops within the walls of a town was deemed to be satisfactorily answered provided a stream or river flowed through or near the place, and offered a current or tide to wash away, in boundless wastefulness, those matters which, when properly applied, will endow barren lands with the richest fertility. At the present time the ultimate economy of the art of sewerage comprehends two distinct purposes, whereof the second, viz., the disposal and utilization of the refuse matters, is little less in importance than the first, viz., the discharge of these matters from the dwellings and highways of man.

The accomplishment of the second purpose involves the beneficial appropriation of refuse matters so as to make them actually productive, and to avoid interference with those healthy uses of inland waters for which they are by nature adapted. In illustration of this principle, it will not be amiss to estimate (1), the pernicious effects of discharging these matters upon the surface of the earth, or into streams from whence the supply of water is derived for the several uses of communities; and (2), their value for agricultural purposes.

———————

CHAPTER III.

Sewage a Fruitful and Deadly Source of Contamination.

IT is obvious that infection of the soil by decaying organic matters will not only vitiate the subterranean waters, but also the air of dwellings to the extent of impairing health. Independently of the infected volatile products which are evolved in the process of putrefaction, infective germs are sometimes concealed in the excretions, especially the dejections from cholera and typhoid patients.

The accumulation of the refuse matters of every-day life in the neighborhood of human habitations becomes more dangerous in proportion to the quantity accumulated, since the chances of infiltration, with its train of evil consequences, such as vitiated air, polluted soil and contaminated water, are greatly multiplied. Ersmann estimates the poisonous gases eliminated from a ton of excretal sewage—solid and liquid—in 24 hours as follows:

Carbonic Acid...315.0 Liters
Ammonia...149.0 "
Sulphureted Hydrogen..1.2
Hydrocarburets...570.0

which represents a total weight of 1 per cent.

There is a prevailing impression that the germs of typhoid fever are not communicated through the air we breathe, but are transmitted only by the absorption of the water we drink or the food we eat. A great number of observations, however, have shown this opinion to be erroneous, and it is now known that the disease can be communicated through the medium of infected air.

After studying the various ways by which typhoid fever may be propagated, Prof. Bouchard of the Faculty of Paris says:

"The transmission of typhoid fever by polluted air rests "upon evidence the most positive. Gielt relates that a man "who had contracted the disease at Ulme returned to his home, "a village in which the malady had not existed for many years, "and the disease soon developed itself in the town. The dejec-"tions of the sick man were thrown on a manure heap; in a "short time thereafter four persons were attainted with the "disease, and a fifth had intestinal catarrh with tumefaction of "the spleen. The dejections of these new cases were buried "under another manure heap, which was opened after nine "months. Two men were employed at this work and one of the "two contracted typhoid fever and died." *

According to Greisinger, the development of typhoid fever depends upon the action of putrid exhalations, particularly such

* Report of the International Medical Congress of Geneva, September, 1877.

as come from filthy privy pits and from excretal matters under-
going putrefactive fermentation in cesspools and sewers. These
emanations he regards as "the active elements which play the
essential rôle in epidemics of typhoid fever." *

Laver has communicated the following details of a serious
endemic of typhoid fever which occurred in a boys' school
attached to a charity institution:

"Of thirty-five pupils twenty-eight contracted the malady.
"The first cases, and at the same time the most serious, occurred
"among the pupils who occupied the benches *a* and *b*, on the
"diagram; and the very first case was that of the pupil who
"sat in the seat indicated by the figure 1. The cases observed
"among the pupils who sat at the desk *c* were relatively mild."

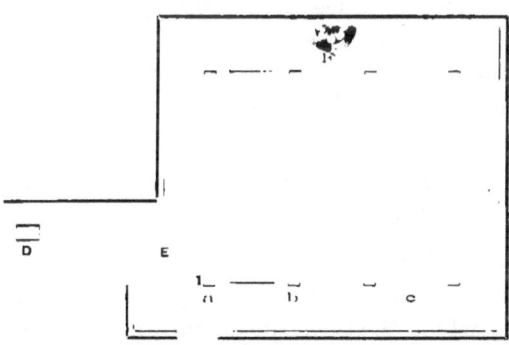

"All the pupils slept in similar apartments, ate the same
"food and, in all respects, were treated alike."

M. Laver was convinced that the fever was caused by emanations proceeding from an open inlet to the sewer, situated in
the passage-way marked D. He says: "It will be noticed that
"the pupils seated on the benches marked *a* and *b*, who were

* *Traité des Maladies Infectieuses*, page 256.

"the most seriously affected, were directly in the current of air
"which came from the sewer-inlet D, through the doorway E
"and passed on to the fire F, which at that time was kept burn-
"ing all day. Subsequently the opening into the sewer was
"closed and the fever did not recur. There was no possibility
"of its having been introduced from without, and no case had
"existed previously in the institution. The pupils first attacked
"had been inmates of the house more than twelve months, and
"had not left the premises a single day during the time. The
"establishment was situated a little outside the town, but the
"sewer communicated with the houses of two or three rich
"families, in each of which there had been several cases of
"typhoid fever."

Murchison (*Treatise on Typhoid Fever*, 1878, pg. 73) relates
the following circumstance: "During the autumn of 1858, an
"epidemic of typhoid fever declared itself at Windsor, which
"was made the subject of special study by a medical commis-
"sion. Four hundred and forty persons were attacked and
"thirty-nine died. The opinion of all who were engaged in the
"investigation was that the fever was due to emanations from
"the sewers, which passed directly into the houses."

In M. Leon Colin's *Study of Typhoid Fever*, (Paris 1878, pg.
109 to 120) he recounts a number of epidemics of typhoid fever,
the origin of which the army physicians ascribed to miasmatic
emanations from latrines and cesspools located in the barracks
or garrison. Many other illustrations might be cited wherein
the outbreak of the disease has been traced directly to the
poisoned air proceeding from sewers and excretal cesspools.

We should hesitate to pronounce as dangerous kitchen
slops and other household waste waters, when recently formed,
and free from putrescent matters or infectious germs; but
Emerich has demonstrated that while such refuse liquids when
fresh cause no injurious effects if injected into the circulation

of animals, they will occasion disastrous effects if injected
after they have remained several days and become decomposed.
It not infrequently happens, moreover, that these foul waters
contain infectious germs, and the necessity of exercising great
care with reference to them is not only important but urgent.

Another evil to be guarded against is the impregnation of
the soil by organic wastes which accumulate in the vicinity of
inhabited places. It is true we cannot always prevent a certain
quantity of household refuse from falling upon and pene-
trating the soil, but it is nevertheless a duty which we owe to the
public health to reduce this source of pollution to a minimum.
To a certain extent the earth possesses the power of disinfecting organic matters, and of destroying pathogenic micro-organ-
isms ; this has been demonstrated in the case of the *comma
bacillus* of Asiatic cholera. But the disinfecting power of the
soil, which varies according to its constitution, its permeability to air and water, its condition of humidity, temperature,
&c.. cannot be relied upon. We find also that the oxydation of
organic matter is more active in proportion as the degree of
saturation is less, and if the soil should receive more material
than it can transform or disinfect, harmless decomposition will
be replaced by obnoxious putrefaction.

All who have witnessed excavations made in proximity
to filthy cesspools or cess-pits must have observed the black and
beslimed condition of the soil, which often emits a disagreeable
odor characteristic of the presence of excrementitious matters.
This condition is influenced by the porosity or permeability of
the soil, and when it exists the saturation does not remain cir-
cumscribed, but the foul liquids continue to penetrate in greater
abundance until they find an impermeable stratum, or a flowing stream which conveys them perchance into some source of
water supply.

Another danger, less apparent but not less formidable, which arises from pollution of the soil by organic matters, is the vitiation of what is known as "ground air." This air, which occupies the interstices of the soil to a depth of several feet, is, especially in the winter when the rooms are warmed, drawn into the apartments and forms part of the ventilation of the rooms, particularly those on the ground floor, which generally contain 10 or 15 per cent. of ground air. One can, therefore, readily understand and appreciate the importance, nay the necessity of preserving the soil near dwelling houses in a pure and uncontaminated condition, for, as is the soil near a dwelling, so will be the air within.

It is manifest that where the disposal of excrementitious matters are not made with proper care, and where the water supply for domestic purposes is drawn from superficial wells, the depth of which seldom reaches more than 20 or 30 feet and rarely exceeds 50 feet, there is great danger of contamination, since the filtering bed through which the refuse liquids percolate and are carried in their course by meteoric waters are insufficient to transform or disinfect all the poisonous organic matters which they contain.

The above diagram illustrates how a well may be contaminated from surface drainage and soakage. Five cases of typhoid fever occurred in the family living in the house, and seven more among other persons using water from the same well.

This condition, important in a sanitary point of view, is characterized by the presence in the water of nitrates, nitrites, ammonia, chlorine, potash and organic matters notably in excess of those found in water drawn from unpolluted wells, or wells situated remotely from any source of pollution. It is quite well kn-°wn to all who have paid attention to such matters, that water may be entirely limpid and tasteless and yet contain the same organic matters which are found in the most offensive liquid sewage.

It appears, moreover, from the evidence of scientific research, as well as from reasoning by analogy, that water may be contaminated by being mixed not only with the organic matter of sewage, but also by passing over or coming in contact with the polluted soil of graveyards, decomposing matters of cesspools and privies, or by the organic matter derived from the decay of any animal or vegetable organisms. But the most dangerous sources of contaminated water are undoubtedly the wells, springs, streams or rivers from which water is used for household purposes, and into which more or less excretal sewage has passed. Numerous cases in proof of this could be cited, but it is only necessary to give the following, which is indicative of general results in similar cases :

Mr. Burns relates that in a certain town of Scotland there was a severe outbreak of dysentery and typhoid fever. A physician called to attend some of the cases, set to work to find out the cause. On inquiry as to the water supply, he was directed to a spring on low ground in the midst of the settlement, so situated as to receive the drainage from a cesspool. The water was pure and sparkling to the sight and taste, and was loudly praised by those who used it. A quantity put in a bottle and allowed to stand a few hours, threw down a thick sediment of most offensive matter, which, on being tested, was found to be as purely excrementitious as if it had been taken from a privy. The people ceased to use this water, and the epidemic disappeared at once.

In a village of New York typhoid fever broke out and prevailed with great violence in a certain locality. Search was made for the cause by the attending physician, but in vain. An appeal was made to the health authoreies, and an expert officer examined the history of the outbreak and predicted that a certain hydrant which supplied the victims with drinking water communicated at some point with house drains or the street sewer. The water-pipe was examined, and at a distance from the hydrant a house drain was found leading into it at a point where they traversed each other. The repair of these pipes was the cure of the epidemic.

In a farmhouse in Massachusetts, situated in an interior township famous for healthfulness and the beauty of its scenery, typhoid fever broke out in a violent form. Of eight members five perished and one was seriously ill. The house was situated on an elevation, and all its surroundings were admirably arranged for health. One could readily believe the statement that "there had not been a case of sickness in the house for twelve years." The following is a history of the sickness: "A few weeks before the disease appeared, the pump in the " well broke, and the farmer being pressed with work, neglected " to have it repaired. Meantime the servants brought water " from a spring at the foot of the hill, which soon became low, " owing to a drought. Resort was then had to a small brook, " and from this source the family were supplied with water for " two weeks. This stream, higher up, ran through several farm " yards, and received the surface drainage. The first symptoms " of poison by this water were slight nausea and a mild diarrhœa.

" After several days typhoid fever in its worst form was ushered
" in. Of the entire family, but two escaped an attack, and
" they did not use the water. An examination of this water
" revealed a sediment of excretal matters."

At Pittsfield, Massachusetts, typhoid fever suddenly broke
out in a large boarding school for young ladies. The water was
found to be contaminated with sewage, owing to leakage from
the cesspool. A similar occurrence took place some years ago
at Princeton College, New Jersey.

At Edgewood, on Staten Island, Prof. Chandler relates that
the inmates of a small block of houses were affected with
typhoid fever, several deaths occurring. On making investigation, it was found that a neighbor through whose land the underground drain passed had taken the liberty of closing up the drain,
thus sending its contents back upon this block of houses, con-
tims taminating the wells, and murdering the unfortunate vic-
with sewage poison.

The process of filtration through the soil, which water
derived from subterranean sources undergoes, tends to separate
the organic impurities, animal and vegetable, but this process
is often palpably insufficient to secure the requisite purity.
The topographical and geological character of the site of the
town, and of the soil and sub-strata, are also to be taken into
consideration.

In speaking of the bored wells on Manhattan Island,
numbering about sixty or seventy, and varying in depth from
twenty-six to two thousand feet, eighteen being more than five
hundred feet deep, Prof. C. F. Chandler states that the water
from such wells can never be free from danger, if drank before
being boiled. " The geological formation," says Prof. Chandler,
" renders it impossible for water to come in from beyond the
" limits of the island, except possibly in one locality, for a short
" distance south of Harlem river. It is only filtered surface

"water, and however clear it may be, it is always in danger of "containing disease germs which cannot be filtered out by the "soil." Prof. Chandler also declares, in a paper on "The Sanitary Chemistry of Water," published in the reports of the American Public Health Association, that "many diseases of the most "fatal character are now traced to the use of water poisoned "with the soakage from soils charged with sewage and excre-"mental matters."

Dr. Macadam, a distinguished chemist of Edinburgh, Scotland, who has paid great attention to the water question, states that, "the line must be distinctly drawn between non-putrescent "organic matter and that which is putrescent. Impregnations "from sewage form the most dreaded contamination, and yield "waters which though clear and sparkling, and cooling and "refreshing, are yet most unwholesome and deadly."

Dr. Frankland maintains that water once contaminated with sewage matter, even if purified subsequently by filtration in the most perfect way attainable, if not positively dangerous, is still unsafe to be used. "There are animal organisms existing "in sewage matter so minute as not to be seen by the unaided "eye: and we have reason to believe that they even exist out-"side the range of microscopic vision and possess powers "antagonistic to human life. By their minuteness they defy "filtration, and such is their tenacity to life that they are said "even to outlive the process of boiling."

The futility of simple filtration has been clearly established by the experiments of Dr. Frankland, which he thus describes: "One volume of the rice-water evacuations of a "cholera patient was mixed with 500 volumes of distilled water "and the mixture passed through filtering paper. Before the "filtration the liquid was opalescent, and so it remained after-"wards. In this state 100,000 parts of the filtered liquid, when "submitted to the action of potassic permanganate, required

".0430 part of oxygen for the oxidation of the organic matter
"contained therein. The average amount of oxygen required
"to oxidize the organic matter contained in 100,000 parts of fil-
"tered Thames water, as supplied to the metropolis, is .0724 part.
"Thus, according to the potassic permanganate test, the diluted
"rice-water was far purer as regards organic matter than the
"water ordinarily drank by the inhabitants of London. In
"fact," says Dr. Frankland, "it may be safely asserted that the
"addition of cholera rice-water to the water of the Thames, in
"the proportion of 1 to 1,000, would not materially affect the
"result of a chemical analysis of the water. The filtered rice-
"water liquid was next passed rapidly through animal charcoal.
"The opalescence was thereby further diminished, but not
"entirely removed. The organic matter still remaining in
"100,000 parts required only .0103 part of oxygen for its oxida-
"tion." Dr. Frankland sums up by saying: "The foregoing
"experiments show, first, that the water may be seriously con-
"taminated with choleraic matter, without the presence of the
"latter being indicated by chemical analysis; and, secondly, that
"water so contaminated is not completely deprived of this
"impurity either by filtration or passage through animal char-
"coal."

Experiments by Prof. Thiersch and Dr. Saunderson show
that paper saturated in cholera flux and dried, when eaten will
produce the disease in a transmissible form in mice. "The fresh
"flux the first day after exposure in the air is almost inert, on
"the second day it grows more active, on the third it is at its
"maximum of activity, is less and less active on the fourth and
"fifth, and becomes inert on the sixth day of transformation.
"Of 148 mice experimented on, 95 showed no symptoms, 53
"were affected, and of the latter 31 died. It is remarkable that
"on a second occasion, when the thermometer had fallen from
"56° to 49°, the experiments failed. One circumstance which

"increases the danger is the law observed by cholera, in common
"with other zymotic diseases, whereby the mildest type is
"capable of communicating the disease in its most malignant
"form. Thus the most virulent cholera matter is producible
"from patients who are seemingly only attacked with diarrhœa.
"Experience also shows that water poisoned by sewage is
"capable of propagating cholera, even though the water be
"boiled and drank in the form of tea."

Cholera flux is represented to be of low specific gravity, and
sinks very slowly in water. Dr. Hassall describes the deposit,
when seen under the microscope, as consisting of "innumerable
"mucous corpuscles, globules of oil, and myriads of vibriones."
Pacani has found that the germs of vibriones are less than the
25,000th of an inch in diameter; so that if heaped in a mass,
there would be as many as 15,625,000,000,000 germs in a cubic
inch. "Allowing for interspaces," says Dr. Farr, "it is evident
"that a cubic inch might hold millions of cholera particles, and
"one cholera patient might disseminate in water millions of
"zymotic molecules. The infective power of the cholera liquid
"grows and declines by a law of its own; and the water which
"on one day is poisonous, may a few days afterwards be
"harmless." The occurrence of the vegetable species and ani-
malculae is, says Dr. Hassall, "an infallible proof of the pres-
"ence of organic impurity in its worst stage,—that is, in the
"act of putrid decomposition, or in the course towards this
"consummation."

Such is the nature of the influence which may be said to
threaten the water supply of some of our Maryland towns.
The analysis of waters from several of the wells of Towsontown
made by Prof. Tonry for the State Board of Health, during the
existence of typhoid fever in that place, showed the presence of
nitrates and a considerable amount of organic matter, and we
cannot be assured that animal organizations of a dangerous

type will not sometimes accompany these compounds. And what is true of the water supply in Towsontown is equally true of most of the towns and villages in the State. Certainly, taking all things into consideration, it appears to be unmistakably a wrong thing to draw the water for house consumption from wells or any other source of supply into which sewage matters are passed. Clearly, the utmost care ought to be taken to exclude impure fluids and other offensive matters from every water supply, and in most of our towns this can only be effected by providing a proper system of sewage disposal. "For health's "sake, without consideration of commercial profit, sewage and "excreta should be got rid of at any cost."

CHAPTER IV.

REDUCTION OF MORTALITY FOLLOWING THE INTRODUCTION OF SEWERS.

THE great importance of avoiding all sources of unwholesome and offensive effluvia, and of preserving the foundations of buildings, and the substrata of the soil of a town in a dry and clean condition, creates a severe necessity for relinquishing cesspools and all receptacles for sewage within or connected with buildings, except those to which the material is conducted for purposes of collection and treatment.

The advantages to be derived, in a sanitary point of view, and the great reduction in the annual mortality of towns from the construction of an efficient system of sewers, has been strikingly set forth by Capt. Douglas Galton, of the Royal Engi-

neers, in an address before the Sanitary Institute of Great
Britain, from which the following extracts are taken:

"It may be accepted as certain that in every case where
"the sewage of towns has been devised on sound principles, and
"where the works have been carried on under intelligent super-
"vision, a largely reduced death-rate has invariably followed.
"The records of Newcastle afford evidence of this fact. The
"quinquennial period beginning in 1868 showed a death-rate of
"27.6; the quinquennial period ending in 1881 showed a death-
"rate of 23.0; whilst the death-rate of 1881 was only 21.7."

"At the recent Sanitary Congress at Vienna, some remark-
"able results of the effects of the sewerage of certain German
"towns were given, which are very striking."

"Munich is the residence of one of the ablest sanitarians of
"Europe, Dr. Pettenkofer. His admirable illustrations of the
"effect of the impurities which were accumulated in porous
"cesspits upon the air of the town, and the death-rate of the
"population, form a text-book of sanitary knowledge."

"At Munich, the enteric (typhoid) fever mortality *per*
"100,000 *of inhabitants* per quinquennial periods was as under:

    1854 to 1859, when there were absolutely no regulations for
        keeping the soil clean.. 24.2
    1860 to 1865, when reforms were begun by cementing the sides
        and bottoms of the porous cesspits................................. 16.8
    1866 to 1873, when there was partial sewerage 13.3
    1876 to 1880, when the sewerage was complete....................... 8.7

"Similarly at Frankfort-on-Main, the deaths from enteric
"fever *per* 10,000 were:

    1854 to 1859, when there was no sewerage............................. 8.7
    1875 to 1887, when the sewerage was complete,...................... 2.4

"At Dantzic, the figures present some striking character-
"istics; the deaths from enteric fever *per* 100,000 *living* was as
"follows:

1865 to 1869, when there was no sewerage and no proper water
supply 108
1871 to 1875, after the introduction of water supply................. 90
1876 to 1880, after the introduction of sewers......................... 18

"Hamburg has been drained by Mr. Lindley, and he has
"stated that in his plans he carefully followed the principles
"laid down by Mr. Chadwick. In that town, the deaths from
"enteric fever *per* 1,000 of total population were:

From 1838 to 1844, before the commencement of the construction of any sewerage works... 48.5
From 1871 to 1880, after the completion of the sewerage works.. 13.3

"During the time that the works were in progress, viz: from
"1872 to 1874, the mortality from enteric fever *per* 10,000 *living*
"was:

In the unsewered districts.. 40.0
In the districts for the most part sewered 32.0
And in the fully sewered districts. 26.8

Dr. Buchanan, Medical Officer of the Privy Council of
England, in his Ninth Report has shown the marked improve-
.ment to health which followed the introduction of drainage,
sewerage and water supplies, in twenty-five cities and towns,
with an aggregate population of 593,736 persons. The average
of the death-rates per 10,000 for the different places decreased as
follows:

Mortality from all Causes..............................from 247.55 to 219.87
"   "   Typhoid Fever...................... "   13.34 "   7.8
"   "   Diarrhœa............................ "   8.45 "   7.66
"   "   Pulmonary Consumption.......... "   34.44 "   27.3
"   Among Children under 1 year old...... "   55.65 "   50.00

In some of these towns it was clearly demonstrated that
improperly constructed sewers had increased the death-rate, by
exposing people to the direct effect of deleterious gases.

These results illustrate the effects of purifying the air of
towns by the rapid abstraction of refuse matter, so as to pre-

vent it from remaining and putrefying in and upon the ground. These figures show a reduction in the death-rate of the above towns from typhoid fever alone of fully 24 per cent., and it is fair to presume that diphtheria and other zymotic miasmatic fevers would be similarly affected.

It may, therefore, be estimated that in the city of Baltimore (where there are, according to the last Report of the Health Department, 1,780 deaths annually from such diseases), about 500 persons who now die of these diseases would be saved from death every year if the city were properly sewered; and if twelve cases of serious, but not fatal illness be reckoned for every death, it follows that about 6,000 persons would be saved from a sick-bed through the influence of this sanitary measure alone, while the saving to the body politic may be estimated in figures as follows:

500 funerals at an average cost of $30 each......................	$ 15,000
6,000 cases of sickness at an average cost of $15 in each case for medical treatment and other expenses incident to sickness...	90,000
Loss of time, averaging 10 days in each case of sickness, at $2.50 per day per person.......................................	150,000
Total annual loss...;	$255,000

Which sum capitalized at 5 per cent. would amount to more than $4.000,000, or a sum quite equal to the cost of constructing an efficient system of sewers.

Concerning the benefits derived in England, for the decennial period 1870–1880, from sanitary measures the Local Government Board thus speaks:

"On the demonstrations of various model instances, it may "be held that the reduction of the general death-rate (three-"eighths of the entire reduction being in 'fever') by four and "one half per cent., as reported, satisfactory as this is, cannot "be considered more than one-third of the results obtainable

"by advanced sanitary administrations and further sanitary
"works. The pain and misery and the social disorder occa-
"sioned by excessive sickness and premature mortality are
"greatly beyond pecuniary estimation."

"Among the causes," says Mr. Gray, "which have operated
"in England to produce these remarkable results may be men-
"tioned the construction of more perfect systems of sewerage
"and house drainage. the gradual disuse of cesspools and wells,·
"the introduction of more copious water supplies, the more
"efficient seweraging of towns, the sanitary inspection of
"dwellings, and the purification and utilization of sewage."

Although a great deal has been done in Maryland to arouse
the public from their apathy, there is reason to believe that
much indifference still exists. even in the principal cities of the
State, upon the subject of sanitary reform, and that the people
are too much inclined to overlook the evils which surround
them. How long the problem of sewering the city of Baltimore,
the solution of which is not by any means overwhelming, will
be permitted to rest unattacked may possibly only be determined by the occurrence in the future of an epidemic deci-
mation, giving the neccessary stimulus to more advanced
metropolitan sanitary legislation, thereby removing what now
exists as a blot upon the cleanliness of one of the largest and
most beautiful cities in the country.

CHAPTER V.

Composition and Manurial Value of Sewage.

IT is quite impossible to estimate with precision the amount of excretal matter which is produced daily by a mixed population, composed of persons of all ages and conditions. The estimate to be accurate should be made for each particular case, since the amount will necessarily vary with age and the conditions of life, viz., the amount of food, the consumption of water, &c We can, therefore, only take as a basis of calculation the average of different authors.

The quantity of solid excreta yielded per day by each individual, taking all classes and all ages together, is estimated by Parks at 75 grammes (2½ oz.) of fæces and 1,200 grammes (40 oz.) of urine per day. Frankland concurs with Parks as to the amount of urine, but he estimates the quantity of fæcal matter at 90 grammes (3 oz.) Pettenkofer fixes the amount of solid matter at 93 grammes (3¹⁄₁₀ oz.) and the urine at 1,172 grammes (39⅔ oz.) per day per person. Averaging the figures of the three above authorities we find that the fæces amount to 2⅔ oz., and the urine to 39¾ oz. per day per person, which may be regarded as correct. Pettenkofer further estimates that house and kitchen wastes will average 223 grammes (7½ oz.) per head per day, or about 165 pounds per person per year. The household waters he fixes at 5 gallons per day, or in round numbers at about 2,000 gallons per person per year.

In America, where water is more lavishly used, these figures may be doubled if not quadrupled.

A special commission of sanitary experts, consisting of Messrs. Royers, Devaugh and Putzeys, have recently made a report to the Royal Society of Public Medicine of Belgium on the removal of excrementitious matters from centres of population, in which it is stated that the refuse household materials, liquid and solid, which has to be removed from habitations, represents per head and per year a total of 7.852 kilograms, or about 17,275 pounds, into which there enters:

Solid fæcal matter.. 0.45 per cent.

Urine.. 5.45 " "

Products of house waste..................................... 1.15 " "

Refuse waters.. 92.97 " "

The Commission further estimates that for each 1,000 of population there will be:

34 cubic metres (tons) of fæcal matter.

428 " " " urine.

7.300 " " " soiled waters.

90 " " " house waste.

It is quite impossible, says the Report, to estimate the volume of industrial waters, since the quantity used in each instance varies with the nature of the industry.

Industrial wastes, however, are not to be neglected; on the contrary, it is very desirable, in a sanitary point of view, that their proper disposal be provided for. Certain industries, such as slaughter-houses, tanneries, manufactories of cloths and chemicals, sugar refineries, glue factories, rendering and dyeing establishments, &c., produce wastes which are particularly objectionable, since they readily pass into a state of fermentation and putrefaction, and become a fruitful source of danger to public health.

The following table, taken from the Report of the Rivers' Pollution Commission of England, gives the average composition of sewerage in parts per 100,000:

DESCRIPTION.	Solids In Solution.	Organic Carbon.	Organic Nitrogen.	Ammonia.	Nitrogen as Nitrates.	Total Combined Nitrogen.	Chlorine.	SUSPENDED MATTERS.		
								Mineral.	Organic.	Total.
WATER CLOSET—										
Towns	72.2	4.696	2.205	6.703	.003	7.728	10.66	24.18	20.51	44.69
MIDDENS—										
Towns	82.4	4.181	1.975	5.435	.000	6.451	11.54	17.81	21.30	39.11

Messrs. Schlœsing and Durand-Claye, after ten years of careful investigation, furnish the following analysis, per cubic metre (ton) of sewage water, taken from the outfall sewers of Paris:

Nitrogen 45 grms.		
Other volatile or combustible matters (principally organic) 678	723 grms.	
Phosphoric acid 19		2908 grms.
Potash 37		
Lime 401		
Soda 85	2185	
Magnesia 22		
Insoluble matters (principally selicious) 728		
Mineral matters 893		

The municipal engineers of Paris have ascertained that from 250,000 to 260,000 cubic metres (tons) of this impure water are emptied daily into the Seine from the "collecteurs" or intercepting sewers, and this amount constitutes about 70 per cent. of the daily water supply of the city, the remaining 30 per cent. being disposed of by evaporation. Two-thirds of the matters contained in these sewer waters, i. e., 1,940 grammes of the 2,908 are solid matters, and formed for the most part of sand, or debris washed from the streets. The dissolved materials, i. e., 968 grammes of the 2,908, contain one-half of all the nitrogen and organic matters, and all the potash.

The sewer waters of London have less solid material, but are richer in nitrogen than those of Paris. According to the analysis of Frankland they contain on an average, *per cubic metre*, 643 grammes of solid material (three times less than the sewer waters of Paris) and 64 grammes of dissolved material. These elements are given as follows:

Nitrogen	dissolved	organic, 25 grms.	71 grms.		
		as ammonia, 46		80 grms.	
	contained in the solids...........	9			1288 grms.
Organic carbon..................................	44				
Chlorine...	104		1208		
Other dissolved matters........................	426				
Other matters in suspension..................	634				

The analysis of mixed gases obtained from sewer mud by M. Charles Girard, Director of the Laboratory of the Prefect of Police of Paris, gives the following result:

Sulphuretted hydrogen....................................	0.96
Carbonic acid...	9.60
Oxygen	0.96
Protocarbonate of hydrogen and nitrogen...............	88.40
Total...	100.00

But if we examine the chemical composition of excrementitious matters alone we shall find, according to the Report of the Belgian Commission, that the faeces contain about 75 per cent. of water, 1.2 to 2 per cent. of nitrogen and 3.25 to 3.75 of combustible matters, which furnish 1.6 per cent. of phosphoric acid, 0.29 per cent. of potash and 1.4 per cent. of nitrogen. The last three substances merit especial attention on account of their great importance in agriculture.

The composition of urine is more variable than that of the faeces:—The proportion of water varies between 93.3 and 96 per cent.; that of nitrogen between 1.2 and 2.6 according to the food; the quantity of phosphoric acid and of potash are each 0.2 per cent.

It appears from the foregoing figures that one person will, on an average, excrete annually with the fæces from 1 to 1½ pounds of nitrogen, and with the urine from 10 to 12 pounds; 13 ounces of phosphoric acid are excreted with the fæces, and 2 pounds with the urine of each person annually; and if we consider that the fermentable principle of excrementitious matters resides principally in the nitrogenous substances which they contain, and that it is from this source more particularly that the pollution of soil, air and water occurs, we can readily understand that the urine is in every respect of greater importance than the fæces. This fact being known, attention to conserving the urine both as an economical and health measure should not be lost sight of.

The value of manures as promoters of vegetation is known to result from their possessing the essential element, nitrogen, in the form of ammonia, with the subordinate properties of alkalies, phosphates and sulphates. Now, according to the figures of the Belgian Commission, the quantity of nitrogen contained in the excrements of each person during one year is about 16 pounds, including about 3 pounds of phosphoric acid, and this quantity is sufficient for the supply of 800 pounds of wheat, rye, or oats, and more than is necessary to add to an acre of land, in order to obtain, with the assistance of the nitrogen absorbed from the atmosphere, the richest crops every year. Making reasonable allowance for the reduced quantity produced by children, we shall be safe in assuming that the nitrogen thus resulting from any amount of population is equal to the supply required for affording 2 pounds of bread per diem for every one of its members. Or assuming an average of 600 pounds of wheat to be manured by each individual of the population of Baltimore, and estimating this at 400,000, the manure thus produced would be sufficient to supply a growth of wheat of a total weight of 240,000,000 pounds.

Other authorities variously estimate the manurial value of the excreta voided daily by 1,000 persons, in their natural condition, at from $5 to $10. This is the theoretical side of the question, for its value is dependent upon circumstances more or less numerous. If diluted with the enormous quantity of water with which town sewage is usually diluted in the water carriage sewers, instead of finding that we have a value of $10 or $20 per ton, we will have a value of only a few cents per ton. Again, the manurial value of sewage not only depends upon what, as a fertilizing substance, it is as compared with other fertilizing substances, but upon the facility and costlessness with which it may be transported. We have already stated that the more concentrated a manure is, the more valuable it is, not merely because the whole of it, or nearly the whole of it, goes to the plant's nourishment—no extraneous and valueless matter being mixed up with it—but because of the transport from place to place. Valuable as we all admit farm-yard manure to be, there is a limit beyond which it would cease to be valuable at all, inasmuch as the cost of its transportation would be worth more than its fertilizing value. Not only is the question of relative bulk to be taken into account, but we must also consider whether we can use the bulky manure when and where we require it. The more bulky a manure is, the less manageable it will be, and the less valuable it will be in a practical point of view. Considerations such as these are eminently practical, and will always affect the sewerage question : but it is not possible, under the water carriage system, to lessen the bulk of the resulting sewage to a great extent, if indeed to any extent.

"The question of bulk," says an eminent authority, "is one "to which attention must be paid if we wish to come to a cor-"rect conclusion as to what chances there are of sewage being "used agriculturally, in all cases where made, that is, in the "neighborhood of towns. The fact that after the lapse of so

" many years, so few towns have managed to get rid of their
" sewage in a satisfactory manner, shows, beyond any cavil, that
" there are difficulties in the way of using sewage. And the
" difficulty is—or rather we should say the difficulties are—enor-
' mously increased by the local circumstances of many towns,
" and the character of the land there met with, judged from
" an agricultural point of view." This authority further
says : " Land cannot be obtained of sufficient extent in the
" neighborhood of towns in which the sewage is produced for
" irrigation purposes; and this may safely be accepted as the
" rule, when we consider that one acre is required for every
" twenty or twenty-five individuals of the population. The
" land must, moreover, be of a certain quality, to give the best
" results ; and locally, so far as its surface is concerned, arranged
" in a certain way before the best results of the application can
" be secured. With regard to this point there is, or rather will
" be, if the sewage of large towns is to be used for irrigation, an
" almost insuperable difficulty in getting the requisite quan-
" tity and the proper quality of land for the utilization of the
" enormous quantities produced by the present system of town
" sanitary arrangements," *whereby the excretal matters are discharged into the same channels with the waste waters and all other
matters from the surface of the streets.*

We have seen that the average quantity of excretal matter,
solid and liquid, passed by one person in twenty-four hours
amounts to forty-three ounces. Now the city of Baltimore, with
a population of 400,000, has up to the present time allowed to go
to waste, in round numbers, 200,000 tons of excretal matter annually, which could be converted into a valuable fertilizer. And
as the population of the State of Maryland is about one mil-
lion, there could be preserved upwards of 500,000 tons of excreta
which is now allowed to go to waste. and which, if it were
properly treated, would produce at least 125,000 tons of a valu-

able fertilizer, worth in the aggregate more than $3,000,000.
In addition to this great advantage to the agricultural interests
of the State, the cities, towns and villages would be relieved of
excretal matter, which is now a problem of so much difficulty.

The value of the fertilizing constituents in human excretions are fixed by Goessman as follows:

Nitrogen.......................................15 cents per pound.
Soluble Phosphoric Acid................................12   "   "
Reverted Phosphoric Acid............................. 9   "   "
Potassium Oxide... 7   "   "

In Germany the nitrogen is estimated in the following
manner:

Total Nitrogen, 7.24 per cent. $\begin{cases} 4.49 \text{ per cent. as Ammonia.} \\ 2.75 \text{ per cent. as Organic Combination.} \end{cases}$

VALUE.

Nitrogen as Ammonia.............................24 cents per pound.
   "   " Organic Combinations.................15   "   "

CHAPTER VI.

MODES OF DEALING WITH SEWAGE. CESSPOOLS AND OPEN PRIVIES.

THE refuse matters to be discharged from towns and buildings, consisting of the disintegrated material of streets; of
superfluous rain water; of excrementitious and household
matters, solid and liquid; of the waste products of combustion;
of the refuse of animal and vegetable substances, require
arrangements of different kinds to be provided with regard to
the purposes to which these matters may be usefully applied

In sewerage, as in many other subjects, controversy has frequently been found to be excited upon those very details of the art which appear to be most simple and the most readily deducible from observation, while the proper ground for discussion, in which it is really urgently needed, in order to determine general principles and mark out leading rules, has been left nearly or quite unoccupied. Thus the forms, sizes and thicknesses of sewers have received the most elaborate investigation, and provoked an expression of the most widely different opinions, while the great question of the most healthful and economical disposal of the refuse of towns have, until lately, remained unsought and unasked. "Misled by an instinctive adoption of "obsolete plans," says Mr. Drysdale, "we have been content to "build sewers, patch upon patch,—add length to length of slug-"gish sewer or practical cesspool, without any principle of "arrangement according to which the entire system should be "laid out, in order, it may be, to maintain ancient outfalls."

Reference has already been made to the connection between defective sewerage, or no sewerage at all, and the propagation of disease. It is now universally admitted that the exhalations arising from the decaying putridity of deficiently arranged and constructed cesspools and open privies are strongly inducive of disease. Indeed the immediate and direct cause of zymotic disease may be said to be the poison generated by the decomposition of animal and vegetable matters. The experience of every medical man goes to prove that a badly cleansed and drained district is always an unhealthy one. A competent witness remarks that, "in addition to a general derangement of health, "and an unusual liability to disease, there is one particular class "of disease which is always to be found in neglected places, viz., "the class of contagious disorders." History teaches us that pestilence has always haunted the scenes of filth. The plague, the black death, the cholera, have all made these places their favorite resorts; and typhoid fever and diphtheria, our modern pestilences, form no exception to the rule.

It may be laid down as a great leading principle in the drainage of towns and houses, that *no system for getting rid of human excreta and household waste matters, solid and liquid, can be considered satisfactory which does not provide against vitiation of air, contamination of soil and pollution of drinking water, the most perfect method being that which will provide for the complete, immediate and rapid removal of all waste matters susceptible of decomposition.*

The term "drainage" and "sewerage" are distinct subjects, though, unfortunately, they have come to be used as if they were the same. At one time it was not so. Town drainage, when first introduced, was intended, as it was practically carried out, only as a means of carrying off from the neighborhood of houses the refuse waters of their domestic operations, and for the removal of rain or surface water, and the refuse of manufactories. So completely distinct were they considered from the system of cesspools, that in most places entrance into them from the cesspool was prohibited under a positive penalty ; and further, so distinct were they from any system of sewerage that all excretal matters were forbidden under a penalty to be conducted or thrown into them. The result was, that as the "water closet" became more and more used, and the supply of water to towns was gradually and greatly increased, the "cesspool" system became a greater difficulty than ever, and the evils,—in the form of still more completely saturated soils, polluted wells and foundations, and cellars flooded with stagnant and offensive fluids,—became at last so notorious that a new system became positively imperative, and in place of connections between the water-closets and the storm water drains being rendered a matter of impossility or difficulty the connection was in some instances made imperative. The drains were no longer looked upon as simply a means for conveying the slop water of houses and the surface water of streets, but were made to convey, not only these, but also the excrementitious matter from houses. Formerly they were permeable, not only admitting water draining from the surrounding soil to enter into them, but they acted in the converse way, allowing their contents to pass from their interior and permeate the soil surrounding them. All this was changed. From permeable they were changed to impermeable, so that they were absolutely water-tight, as far as practically possible, in order to retain within their interior the matters which they conveyed, and to prevent as much as possible their passing out to pollute the soil by which they were surrounded.

It will thus be seen that the two systems of old town drains and the new town sewers were specially distinct. In many towns, even in parts of London and Paris, the old drains still remain, being made to serve the purpose of excretal sewers, for which they are quite unfitted, giving rise to evils of a character perhaps less obvious and open to inspection, but not less dangerous than those arising from the old cesspool system. These drains or so-called sewers are but elongated cesspools, and creating, as they must create, a vast amount of foul air in the aggregate, they are certain to act in a way even more dangerous than the old cesspits, for the latter being placed outside the house any foul exhalations from it have the chance of being diffused in the air, or blown away from the neighborhood of the house by favorable winds; whereas, the latter are placed in direct communication with the interior of dwellings by the house soil pipe, so that the foul gases are delivered where they are most dangerous, and must necessarily pass through the house before they escape to the external atmosphere,—if they escape at all. Hence arose the necessity for introducing some means of preventing the gases created in the sewers from passing into the interior of the houses with which they are directly connected. This has been attempted to be effected by what are called " water seals," or in other words " stench traps." By this arrangement the poisonous gases from the interior of the drain are *supposed* to be prevented from passing through the trap, so long as it is completely filled with water.

In the use of the " trap," the gases are " supposed " to be prevented from passing from the drains to the house, but this is not the case, for in many instances the "trap" does not act as such. Its efficiency, at all events, is very doubtful in the generality of cases, since the body of water in the trap or the weight of the "water seal" may be altogether incapable of resisting the pressure of the gases acting upon the drain side of the trap, in which case the gases are simply forced through the trap and pass at once into the house. Nor is this result prevented by extending the soil pipe up to or above the roof level, for often the density of the atmosphere is such that the gases, instead of passing out through the ventilating pipe, will force the "seal " and pass into the house.

In addition, moreover, to the ease with which, under certain circumstances, the gases from the drains and sewers are forced through the small columns of water in the trap, this in certain forms is frequently evaporated, or syphoned, leaving the trap dry, and, of course, in this condition, it is only a trap in name, experience having shown that traps are, in a great many instances, wholly inoperative. A very simple proof of this is open to the inspection of all. Sewage gases are known to contain, as one constituent, sulphureted hydrogen gas: this discolors white lead exposed to its action. Now if the under side of the cover or lid of the water-closet, for example, be painted, and this be closed, the paint becomes, in course of time, quite black; this is caused by the sewage gases being forced through the trap and coming in contact with the paint: if it were not so, the paint would not, ordinarily, become discolored.

In view of the fact that, in a very large number of cases, water-closets and their "traps," as well as the connecting pipes, are defective, and allow readily the escape of gases from drains and sewers into the houses,—gases which are now universally acknowledged to be a prolific cause of typhoid fever, diptheria, and other zymotic diseases,—many plans have been devised to prevent the possibility of their entering the house, such as gully traps, house traps, charcoal traps, swing valves, mercury seals, ventilating closets, disinfectants for neutralizing all effluvia, and a thousand other devices, none of which can be relied upon with any degree of certainty to circumvent the foul emanations. But, as prevention is always better than cure, and however efficient may be the means adopted by which the foul gases generated in, and always present in water-carriage sewers, may be prevented from entering into our houses, or disinfected before they gain access thereto, and, in view of the fact that a large proportion of the defective appliances at present in use, will remain so, it is imperatively necessary that some means should be devised to carry off excrementitious matters and household wastes before fermentative putrefaction takes place, and at the same time to carry off with the material all gases as they are formed, so that they be not allowed to accumulate in the sewers until they become dangerous. Any system that will not accomplish these desiderata is, in a sanitary point of view, absolutely defective.

CHAPTER VII.

EVILS RESULTING FROM THE IMPROPER DISPOSAL OF SEWAGE.

IT cannot be too often repeated that the "water-carriage" plan of *tout a l'egout* is without doubt the worst devised system of sewerage imaginable for getting rid of excrementitious matters, and should the attempt be made to treat the sewage of Baltimore city in this way, it will undoubtedly prove an expensive and fatal blunder. In the first instance, storm water drains receiving the excremental matters of a population, become so many large retorts circulating through the town for the production and distribution of deleterious gases and germs of disease, and in the next place the ultimate disposal of the noxious liquid after it is out of the city is a question which has not been settled in a manner acceptable either to the interests of agriculture or to the laws of hygiene.

Using rivers and estuaries as receptacles for excretal sewage was at first tolerated on the assurance that it would be unrecognizable to the senses, and consequently wholly inoffensive, through the enormous dilution resulting from admixture with the volume of water receiving it, and minute calculations were produced to prove the degree of resulting dilution. Experience, however, has shown that this argument is a fallacy, inasmuch as the mixing in question does not take place at all. The most offensive solid substances float at first on the surface, and, when the water is a running stream, they are soon deposited on the banks as a noxious mud. In speaking of the sewage of the town of Aylesbury, in England, Mr. George Fell, Secretary of the Local Board of Health, gave the following testimony before "The Judicial Committee of Her Majesty's Most Honorable Privy Council." He said: "In 1875 the river "Thame, which is one of the sources of the Thames, at that " time received the sewage of the town, and a portion of it was "carried in undiluted. Out of the sewage of about 4,000 people, " that of about 1.500 was carried in the tanks and there deposited, "and the overflow ran into the river, and this stream got into "such a filthy state that it was a perfect nuisance. It was "practically a sewer ditch. In fact, I myself, when I have had "occasion to be out late of a summer evening or early of a "summer morning have found a kind of fœted miasma per- " vade the whole air. In consequence of the state of the stream " an injunction was applied for by one of the adjoining land- "owners and obtained, and the town was restrained from "pursuing the course that had been adopted hitherto of turning "the sewage undiluted into the stream."

In April, 1882, Mr. George Tatham, Mayor of Leeds, England, testified before the same committee as follows: "I am "Mayor of Leeds, and it is my third year of office. Sometime "ago the Corporation of Leeds was compelled by proceedings " in chancery to purify their sewage before turning it into the "river Aire. We first had complaints in 1855, and we had to "commence some system in 1869 and 1870, under compulsion "from the Court of Chancery. It was not a question of profit, " but a question of doing the work. We were under the direc- "tion of the Court of Chancery to prevent polluted water from "going into the Aire from our sewers, so as not to create a " nuisance."

Captain Burstall, of the Royal Navy, testified before the same committee: "I am secretary to the Thames Conservancy Board. " I knew the Thames and helped to survey it in 1833. It was "surveyed again by the conservators in 1862, about thirty years "afterwards. By comparison of these two surveys, there was

" no difference whatever, scarcely three inches at any place
" between the position of the bed of the river with reference to
" one common datum in thirty years. This was before the
" contents of the sewers ran into the rivers. In 1862 the con-
" tents of the sewers of all London began to run into the
" Thames, part of them at Barking Creek, and part of them at
" Crossness, one being on one side of the river and one on the
" other. Very shortly after this, in a very great number of
" places in the river, large deposits of black sewage mud were
" formed, several of which by my own measuring were from
" eight to twelve feet vertically in thickness. A great quantity
" of organic matter was mixed up with the mud. Red worms
" were also found, not only there, but in the other parts of the
" river as well. Those deposits are due to the matters held in
" suspension in the sewage fluid which is poured into the
" Thames at Crossness and Barking."

Dr. Robert Seely, Health Officer of Aylesbury, states that
since the discharge of sewage into the river which borders that
town has been interdicted, the miasma and fœted odors which
existed have entirely disappeared, and fish have reappeared in
the water. He further states that while the sewage of the
town flowed into the river, epidemics of typhoid fever occurred
from time to time, but since the interdiction of sewage matter,
such epidemics have been unknown.

The average volume of sewage discharged from the houses
and streets of Baltimore, may be roughly estimated at about
15,000,000 gallons daily, containing in suspension about 40 tons,
and in solution about 65 tons of solid matter. Now a portion of
the 65 tons of matter in solution is capable of being precipitated,
and doubtless by the action of oxidation, as well as of actual
precipitation, should it be turned into the fresh water of the
Patapsco river, some portion would actually be so thrown down.
Consequently, it appears that from 50 to 60 tons of objectionable

and putrescent solid matter daily, equalling about 20,000 tons annually, would be admitted into the river and into Chesapeake Bay. The effect of the presence of so large a volume of putrescent matter in the upper bay, placed under conditions favorable for decomposition, can hardly be overestimated. The clothing of the banks of the river and bay with sewage mud, and the mass of gelatinous sewage matter which would accumulate in the bottom of the river and on the shoals of the bay, and which would certainly prove destructive to the fish and oysters, is, apart from the question of sanitation, a convincing proof of the impracticability and folly of ever permitting the sewage of Baltimore to enter Chesapeake Bay.

CHAPTER VIII.

THE PRINCIPLES OF SEWAGE TREATMENT CLASSIFIED UNDER FOUR HEADS.

THE question now arises, how is the sewage of our towns to be treated, as treated it must be, if the health of the inhabitants is to be considered? The methods of treatment or disposal, other than those involved in the system of *tout a l'egout*—sending everything into the sewers—if this indeed may be considered a system at all—and using the sewage in its normal condition and full quantity for the irrigation of land, are pretty numerous and of great diversity of detail, as regards their *modus operandi;* but numerous as they are, they all come under one or other of the following classes :—

1. Keeping the rain and storm waters in drains distinct from those conveying the sewage; the rain water to be passed to river or stream.

2. Dealing with the excreta and household wastes in a special way, altogether separate from the street drains or storm water sewers, leaving these to conduct, in addition to the storm water and street washings, the waste waters of domestic and industrial operations.

3. Precipition or filtration process, by which the solid organic and putrescible portions of the sewage are deposited in a solid form, which can be used as an ordinary manure, passing the liquid portion of it in a condition more or less clear, and free from putrescible matter into rivers and streams, or upon the land.

4. Pneumatic or aspirating process, by which the excrementitious matters and household wastes are forced or drawn through air-tight pipes, as soon as they are formed, by pneumatic suction or pressure, thereby preserving them in a concentrated condition and in a more highly valuable form as a fertilizer after precipitation, as in the 3d process. Thus what is now a nuisance to towns, would become a source of profit to the country generally, and especially to farmers, who would have a valuable manure produced almost at their doors.

CHAPTER IX.

The "Combined" or English "Water-Carriage" System.

THIS system, to which reference has been made in the foregoing pages, exists in nearly all English towns of any size ; also in Paris, Brussels, Hamburg, Frankfort-on-the-Main, and a few other Continental cities. It consists in treating all sewage, rainwater, subsoil-water, household and manufacturing wastes alike, by conducting them jointly off in one and the same conduit, a large volume of flushing water serving as a means of conveyance.

While doubtless it is true, as contended by some of the highest authorities, that the mobile vehicle of water is one admirably adapted to aid in the removal of the sedimentary matter usually contained in sewage water, and that the more water you can send down your drains and sewers, the less chance will there be of their becoming choked up with deposits; still, on the other hand, it is equally true that every addition of the moving or flowing force of the sewage matter, obtained by increasing the quantity of water, must of necessity decrease the value of the sewage as a fertilizer. If the object of our town drainage system were merely to convey away the sewage, the admission of water to act as the moving power might answer the purpose; provided the sewers are kept running *full* all the time, otherwise there must necessarily be more or less sliming of some parts of the wall of the sewer, which will readily decompose in the presence of ample, changing currents of air, affording an admirable nidus for the development and growth of disease germs. Concerning this particular danger, Dr. Von Ovenbeck de Meijer, Professor of Hygiene in the University of Utrecht, Holland, and one of the leading sanitary authorities in Europe, thus pointedly speaks : " I cannot conceive how sanitarians venture to say that "in sewers, *running only* ONE-HALF *full*, containing fæcal mat-"ter, and connected with atmospheric air, there is not a good "condition for the growth of germs of disease, or how engineers "can overlook the fact that the ' water-carriage' system leaves "entirely unsolved the important question : ' What to do with "the sewage without involving danger to health?' Every main "sewer not *completely* and *constantly* filled is dangerous to health ; "and all sewage containing fæcal matter is a danger to health "wilfully created. *Fæcal matter should never be mixed with other* "*wastes in the centre of population.*"

Again, it is obvious that if the object of a town drainage system be to supply us with a fertilizer, in addition to its other objects, the more water we add to the sewers the further we depreciate the value of the fertilizer. Thus, then, we find, that if we advocate the system of water-carried sewage as the correct one, we are placed in a dilemma out of which it is difficult to escape. "If, to keep the sewage matter as strong as possible "as a fertilizer, we do not use much water, then, by the stoppage "of the drains, or at least the sluggish flow through them, we " do not come up to the sanitary requirements of the question : "we make our drains in fact elongated cesspools."

Enough has been said to demonstrate that "water-carriage" sewers, either on the combined or separate plan is not all that could be desired to constitute a reasonably satisfactory result, but we may epitomise the objections to the system as follows :

1. That as a health measure it is now almost universally condemned by sanitarians and medical men, as absolutely and irreconcilably in conflict with the requirements of modern civilization and the teachings of sanitary science.

2. That refuse matters consisting of excreta and household wastes, solid and liquid, to be discharged properly from towns and buildings, require arrangements separate and distinct from the storm water sewers to be provided, both with regard to the health of the community and the purposes to which these matters may be usefully applied.

3. That the system requires a great volume of water for flushing purposes, which does not always exist in towns, and which, in many instances, it is quite impossible to provide.

4. That it presupposes large expenditures in treating the crude sewage, or it is discharged into water courses, or upon open fields, which not only creates an intolerable nuisance, but leaves the ultimate economy of "the art of sewerage,"—the disposal and utility of refuse matters,—uncared for.

5. That where towns are situated at a low level, in relation to the surrounding country, it is quite impossible to give the sewers the requisite declivity for carrying the sewage with sufficient rapidity to prevent their becoming coated with a foul slime, which rapidly enters into putrid fermentation and evolves gases of the most dangerous kind, containing myriads of microscopic organisms, often of deadly fever germs, so extremely light and mobile, that they are liable to be taken up and disseminated through the town by the moisture which rises from the sewers, or to be drawn or forced into our dwellings through water-closet, bath-room and other house connections, put in, it may be, by some "jerry" builder.

6. That in London, where the system exists in its greatest perfection, it has been found to foul both air and water to such an extent that some supplementary arrangement is deemed necessary, and propositions to this end are now being discussed.

In Paris, where the water-carriage system prevails, the almost constant existence of typhoid fever in an epidemic form has determined the Municipal Council to study what measures can be taken to purify the city, and they have experimented with what is known as the Berlier pneumatic system, which is already in operation in a large area of the city, including the district of the Madeleine and extending from the Place de la Concorde to Levallois-Perret.

The *Pall Mall Gazette* in discussing the subject of the Paris sewers, with reference to the incidence of typhoid fever in that city says:

"It is painfully evident to all persons who have studied the "question that energetic measures must be adopted to preserve "the health of the residents and visitors to Paris. Even the "French press, though not prone to discuss such practical and "prosaic subjects, has taken the matter in hand; and 'Les "Odeurs de Paris' is not only the title of a witty pamphlet by

" M. Francique Sarcey, but has served as the heading for many
" a newspaper article. Without entering into technical details or
" elaborate statistics, two or three broad facts will demonstrate
" how grave the danger has become. Thus, it is calculated that
" from 1869 to 1874 the proportion per 100,000 inhabitants who
" died from typhoid fever, diphtheria, small pox, measles and
" scarlet fever amounted to 150.9 ; but this figure has steadily
" increased, and for the years 1879 to 188) had more than dou-
" bled, the proportion being 334.0. Typhoid fever and diphtheria
" were the principal causes of this mischief, and it may be noted
" that the death rate from typhoid fever among French soldiers,
" amounting to 3.3 per 1,000, is the highest recorded in any
" European army. In Paris this fever has become an endemic
" complaint, killing about a thousand persons a year, except
" when it assumes epidemic violence, as in 1876, when 2032 per-
" sons died of typhoid."

In 1880 and 1881 there were more than two thousand deaths
from the same cause, and in 1882 more than three thousand inhabitants fell victims to this preventable disease. The greatest
evils arise from the barbaric system of drainage, the absence of
knowledge as to traps, intercepting, ventilating, &c. There are
in Paris 80,000 cesspools, of which only about 60,000 are emptied
in the course of the year. All the vegetable matters and household waters drain into the sewers, and there are some 17,000
tinettes filtres which, while retaining solids, allow the liquids
to escape into the sewers.

The vast dimension of some of the Paris main sewers does
not prevent their being denounced on all sides as utterly un-
suited for the work to be performed. The fall is insufficient,
the water supply inadequate, the solid deposits are so numerous
that an army of nearly 1,000 men has to be employed to push
the matter along. To drain everything into sewers thus constructed is extremely dangerous. Some of the heavier sew-

age may remain several weeks in these underground passages
before it reaches the outlet, fermenting the while and evolving
gases that can enter without let or hindrance private dwellings. The city has nearly 800 miles of subterranean pipes, of
which about 500 miles are sewer pipes. The largest of these sewers
were constructed at a cost of not less than $60 per running yard ;
the medium size from $40 to $50 per yard ; while the smallest
cost from $15 to $20 per yard. The maintainance of these sewers,
with 940 "egoutiers," or sewer cleaners. 20 boats and 50 wagons,
cost annually $75,000. The maintainance of the sewers and the
cleaning of the public ways of Paris figure in the annual
municipal appropriations at nearly $5,000,000.

Of course the smaller cities of France are not able to sustain
expenditures proportionate to those of Paris, and, consequently,
they are all deficient or absolutely wanting in sewers. Marseilles
(population 320,000) had no sewers forty years ago. The rain
and household waters ran along the streets and emptied into the
old harbor ; recently, and under the pressure of epidemics, canals
have been constructed which convey the sewage waters some
distance from the heart of the city. ·Bordeaux (population
225,000) has only thirty-two miles of sewers in a length of 140
miles of streets. Toulon (population 70,000) has scarcely a
vestige of sewers.

It is not to be expected that the smaller towns can bear the
burthen of an elaborate system of underground sewers, of which
the cost of construction is necessarily very great ; but other
methods have been devised to meet the difficulty.

CHAPTER X.

THE DRY EARTH CLOSET.

OF the systems which propose to deal with excreta in a special way, apart altogether from the liquid refuse of houses, or the storm water and street refuse, a well-known example is that of the Dry Earth Closet. The deodorizing and absorbent power of dry earth or coal ashes has long been known, but a systematic mode of applying it to the treatment of the excreta of houses is due to the Rev. Mr. Moule, who has introduced several mechanical arrangements by which they can be used. The general principle of these is a receptacle for holding the supply of pulverized earth or coal ashes, a contrivance being attached to it by which, after using the closet, a portion of the dry material is made to cover the excreta. However efficient as a deodorizer and absorbent of fæcal matter dry earth may be—although it is very far from being as efficient an agent in this respect as it is by some maintained to be—it is obvious that there are almost insuperable difficulties attendant upon its use on the large scale, which must prevent it from ever being adopted by towns. There are, moreover, other difficulties attendant upon the use of Moule's apparatus, which will retard its very general introduction even in *country* districts, or for small aggregations of population. The quantity of dry earth required for each time the closet is used is very considerable, and the difficulty is still further increased by the fact that the earth requires to be well dried and in a state of fine division.

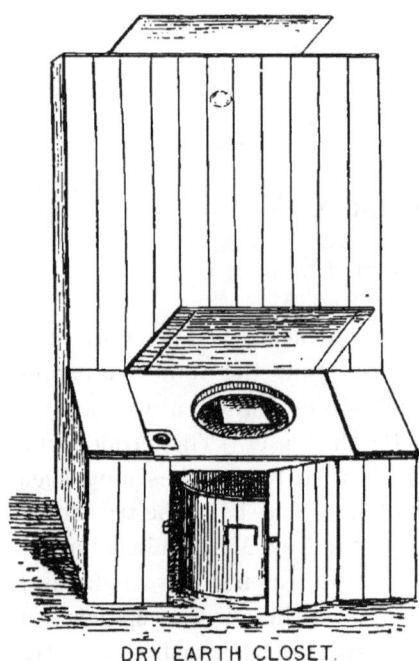

DRY EARTH CLOSET.

The mechanical arrangement of the closet is also such, that the covering of the excreta is not always secured; nor is the value of the manure anything like so high as was at one time supposed. This has been conclusively proved by the experiments published a few years ago by Dr. Voelcker in the *Journal of the Royal Agricultural Society of England.* The Diagram is a representation of the earth closet now generally used in this country. The upper portion, or back, is the Earth or Ash Receiver, the lower part beneath the seat contains a galvanized iron pail. The use of earth-closets at the Maryland Hospital for the Insane, adopted after a large sum had been expended on account of litigation for pollution of a neighboring stream, has not proved satisfactory. The closets are near windows, and when the latter can be kept open and the former are well attended to, there is no serious offence in the wards. At other times the odor is perceptible to quite a distance. The use of a sufficient amount of earth of proper quality is often neglected, and the waste from bath-tubs, etc., is so polluting to the stream into which it is discharged, that complaints are still constantly being made.

Mr. Sandford, of England, claims to have overcome the · objections to the ordinary earth-closet by his "Carbon Closet."

In this the mechanical arrangements are so well devised that the excreta are covered by the deodorizing material with absolute precision and accuracy; and the material employed is dry pulverized charcoal obtained from sea-weed, of which very little is required for each use of the closet. It is also a manurial substance of considerable value when used by itself; but when mixed with the excreta its value as a manure is much increased.

CHAPTER XI.

THE MANCHESTER SYSTEM.

IN the large and densely populated City of Manchester, England, the local peculiarities rendered an adoption of the water closet system on the complete scale, a practical impossibility, not merely from the fact that the necessary supply of water could not at any cost be obtained, but because there was no river near into which the sewage could be discharged, without making it absolutely intolerable from its filthy condition, a condition bad enough at the best under ordinary circumstances. A modification of the "midden and privy system," universally used in the city, was therefore necessitated.

It consists as shown in the diagrams of a common privy, with a small covered ashpit, from the top of which a ventilating shaft is taken to the roof of the house to which it is attached. The floor of the ashpit is of glazed earthenware absolutely water-tight and its door, which is either at the side or back, is kept

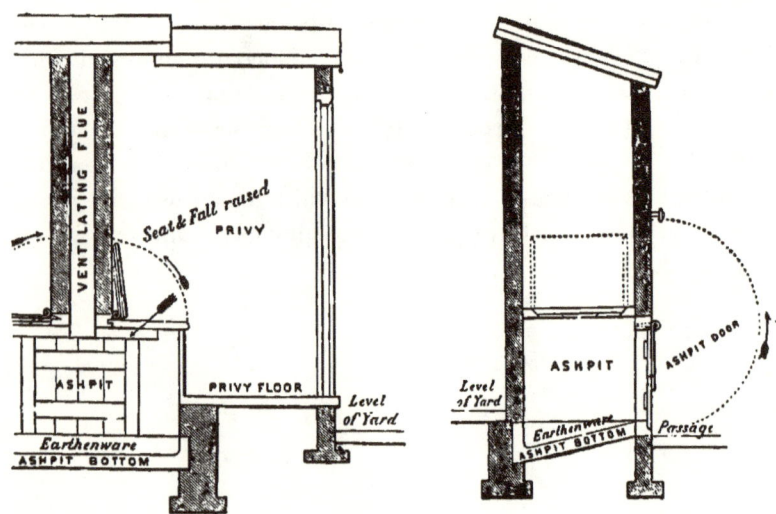

locked, and only opened by the night soil men when they come to empty it. The ashes can only be emptied into the ash pit through the privy seat, (which is provided with hinges and can be raised entirely for this purpose) and must of necessity be poured over the fæcal matter by hand whenever the privy is used.

The receptacle for excrement is of galvanized iron 15 inches high, 18 inches wide and of a capacity of 10 gallons. The matter is removed weekly for most families, twice or thrice a week for very large ones, fortnightly for very small and neat ones. The addition of dry coal ashes is an improvement, but the metal pail is inferior to the strong wooden one made from the kerosene barrel, such as is used at Rochdale; and the sinking of the pit, in which the Manchester pail stands, below the surface of the ground, is objectionable, as it makes removal more difficult.

Boxes are provided for the miscellaneous solid house refuse, and the house slops and liquid refuse are poured into the sewers through a properly trapped grid in front of the dwelling, and a further improvement is also sometimes adopted by which all continuous communication between the house drains and sewers is cut off, and an escape of sewer gas into the interior is made impossible. The ventilation of the sewers is effected by the down-spouts of the houses, and by street gratings left open for the purpose. The "fall" of the sewers and the consequent discharge of the sewage being so rapid no flushing, as a regular system, is required, although it is occasionally carried out. The escape of sewage gases from the interior of the ordinary drains to those of the houses with which they are connected, is prevented by an ordinary trap.

CHAPTER XII.

The Rochdale System.

THE system adopted at Rochdale proceeds upon the same principle as that used in Manchester, the object being the conversion of the old and dangerous system of privy pits into privies calculated to promote health and decency, and keep out from the sewers as much of the excremental matter of the population as possible.

Beneath each closet seat a receptacle, containing a small quantity of a chemical disinfecting fluid is placed, in which the faeces and urine are collected, the vessels being removed in a covered cart in the day-time to a manure manufactory, weekly—or more frequently, if required—an important feature of the process being a retardation of fermentation, so as to prevent the excreta from fouling the atmosphere and being depreciated in value as a manure, which is effected by frequent removal of the receptacles prepared as above stated. The cinders and dry refuse from the house are in like manner collected in common barrels or other receptacles, and, when full, the contents are tipped into a corporation cart and removed to the same depot or manufactory as the excreta, where they are sifted by a winnowing machine, which separates the cinders, refuse vegetable matter, and fine ashes. The vegetable matter is burnt, and its ash and the fine coal ash are used in the manufacture of the manure. There is a ready sale for the large cinders at the price of three shillings a ton, and the smaller cinders are used for working the engine at the manufactory. The fine coal and vegetable ash is mixed with the excreta from the prepared receptacles, the mixture is subjected to a chemical process, and, after being allowed to remain in heaps for a period of about twenty-one days, is passed through a screen to ensure perfect mixing. It is then a damp manure, containing the constituents of the faeces and urine, except a large portion of the water.

By this method of collecting and treating the night soil and refuse of towns there is nothing lost: all is made available, the cinders being found sufficient to raise steam for any motive power required in the process of preparing the manure, and other refuse can be disposed of for their usual purposes. The urine from the public urinals and from dwelling houses, &c., is evaporated and added to the prepared manure. The blood from the slaughter-houses is also, by a simple and inoffensive process, brought into a state fit to be added to the prepared manure, and forms a valuable addition to it. The privies are clean and inodorous, and the plan is certainly a great sanitary and economical improvement over the old privy-pit system.

ROCHDALE PAIL CLOSET.

A. excrement pail.

B. ash tub.

C. seat cover (raised).

D. iron collar below seat, reaching slightly into pail when cover is down.

F. hinged upright of seat.

G door admitting from outside to excrement pail.

Referring to the Manchester and Rochdale systems the Birmingham Sewage Inquiry Committee appointed some years ago to investigate the whole subject with reference to providing a better plan for the sewerage of Birmingham, submitted the following as their general conclusions :

" 1. That the privy-pit system in towns or densely popu-
" lated districts is universally condemned on account of the pol-
" lution of the earth, air, and water in their vicinity, which is
" its inevitable result, and that it is essential to the health,
" cleanliness and comfort of the inhabitants of such districts
" that all fæcal matters should be removed with the greatest
" possible dispatch.

" 2. That this can be effectually done by the Rochdale,
" Manchester or other systems which not only secure the speedy
" removal of these matters, but effectually exclude both their
" solid and liquid constituents from the storm-water sewers.

" 3. That some such system as the Manchester and Rochdale
" system is preferable to the water-closet system where there is
" a difficulty of dealing with the sewage at the outfall.

" 4. That the Rochdale system appears preferable to the
" Manchester system, because it deals separately with the excreta
" and dry refuse, and renders possible the most perfect and
" economical utilization of each.

" 5. That the refuse from slaughter-houses, public urinals,
" and cattle markets may be advantageously collected and
" utilized, &c."

CHAPTER XIII.

THE ORDINARY PRIVY PIT.

THE rudest form of domestic accommodation is an open privy pit over a cesspool, such as is used in the City of Baltimore and every village in Maryland. It deserves notice only on account of its dangers and imperfections. These pits or cesspools are almost universally constructed so that their contents drain into and ooze through the surrounding soil, until the whole neighborhood becomes fully saturated with the drainage, which too often finds its way into the water of springs and wells used for domestic purposes, or through some defective foundation, poisoning, it may be, the basement of an adjoining house.

Cesspools constructed of hard brick or masonry and thoroughly cemented, will prevent this saturation, in proportion as their walls are carefully and imperviously built; but the matters daily discharged into such depositories accumulate, and their decomposition is constantly proceeding, and engendering gases of the most noisome and pestilential kind. The open privy formed over a pit of this description affords an outlet for the escape of these gases, which readily and regularly pass into buildings adjacent to or near the privy; or should a water closet connection be made with the privy through the medium of the soil pipe, the effluvia from the cesspit will pass through the pipe into the house, unless the trap is kept well filled with water; and moreover, the supply of water to the water closet will greatly augment the bulk of the sewage, and necessitate the emptying of the privy much more frequently than otherwise, unless some defects in the joints of the work afford a passage for the liquid matters into the surrounding strata, or a communication be made with a drain. These cesspools are at intervals emptied, but never cleaned; the so-called "cleaning" being more a term used than an operation performed.

It is to be hoped that the public mind in every town and village of our State will soon become impressed with the fact that these cesspits give rise to evils of the gravest character, as influencing in a very marked degree the health of those subjected to them; and that it is necessary to introduce a system more in accordance with sanitary requirements and the civilization of the age.

Another point of great importance in connection with cesspools and open privies, with saturated soil surrounding them, is their bearing upon the supply of pure air to our houses. It is easy to perceive that, however well ventilated our apartments may be, the appliances are rendered futile from the admission of tainted air and by the admixture of gases emanating from filthy accumulations of the cesspool and privy. With reference to the impairment of health from this cause, there is no doubt that it is one of the sources which is absolutely necessary to remove, before there can be any effectual cure. Some of the cesspools are in the cellars, and give out their exhalations from thence; others are in a yard, it may be close to a door or window, and the smell from them is often so noxious as to be unbearable. It not unfrequently happens that the occupants of houses thus located have to remain closely shut up, no air being allowed to enter by door or window, on account of the bad smell which comes from the yard.

But if the "mistakes of our forefathers" must still be tolerated, it will be well, at least, to consider how the evil may be measurably mitigated. This is to be accomplished only by proper construction and vigilant supervision. In the first place, the pits should be constructed according to prescribed rules, and maintained under official inspection. Under no circumstances should they be permitted to be placed within the walls of a building, but as far from the dwelling as practicable, and so constructed as to prevent absolutely any filtration into the subjacent soil. They should be conical in form, or at least built without angles, and smaller at the bottom than the top, of such dimensions as will insure against any large accumulation of matter, ventilated by a pipe extending above the building, and provided with an opening outside the privy house, in order that they may be the more easily emptied. The walls of the pit should be at least twelve inches in thickness, laid of hard brick or masonry, in best hydraulic cement, well puddled with clay on the outer side, and cemented, with smooth finish on the inner side to facilitate scraping and washing whenever emptied. The bottom should be of solid slate or masonry laid upon a substantial cemented foundation.

The process of emptying and cleaning the pits is not only troublesome, but, unless properly performed, will occasion great nuisance; it should, therefore, be done at public rather than individual expense, inasmuch as individuals are prone to sacrifice public health and comfort to private interests; but, if this is not deemed practicable or desirable, then the work should be done under strict official supervision, in order to insure the most thorough and efficient cleansing possible.

CHAPTER XIV.

RECEPTACLES OF SPECIAL CONSTRUCTION.

METALLIC RESERVOIRS. It being very difficult to maintain brick or masonry pits sufficiently secure to prevent
leakage, it has been attempted to overcome this difficulty by
constructing them of iron. When of small dimensions they
may be cast in one solid piece, either tubular or rectangular in
shape, but should it be necessary to have them quite large they
can be constructed of galvanized sheet iron plates securely
riveted. They may rest upon the surface or be sunk below the
soil, but in either event they should rest upon a secure and
unyielding foundation, and be ventilated by a special pipe,
unless the soil pipe of the house extends above the level of the
roof, which is the case with all houses having water closets in
Baltimore. These receptacles occupy much less space than the
ordinary pits constructed of brick or masonry, and one reservoir
may be arranged to receive the outfall pipes from a number of
houses. A reservoir of 65 gallons is capable of receiving daily
during ten days 3½ gallons of dejections and as much water.
Now as one individual will furnish 40 ounces of urine and 3
ounces of fæcal matter in 24 hours, the reservoir will be sufficient for the excreta of nine persons during ten days, one-half the
capacity being occupied by excreta and the other half by water.
Each reservoir should be provided with an automatic register
or index to indicate when it requires to be emptied. The process
of emptying is very simple, being performed readily by the
ordinary excavator or pneumatic pump. This arrangement
has been used quite extensively in some of the German towns

and in St. Petersburg, and, in a somewhat modified form, it was recommended by "The Commission on the Sewerage of Paris" in 1881 (of which commission the *savants* Pasteur and Brouardel were members); but it has never been applied in Paris, on account of the expense involved, which is represented to be very great in large cities where the reservoirs have to be frequently emptied.

THE GOLDNER SYSTEM.—Excretal matter having a density greater than water, M. Goldner, of Baden Baden, has endeavored to utilize this fact by constructing an apparatus in which the excreta will be excluded from contact with atmospheric air by being carried directly under water by gravitation.

A reservoir is constructed of brick or masonry, into which the excremental matter is carried under a bed of water, and remains below until all or most of the water contained in the reservoir is displaced by the liquid and solid excreta, after which the latter is discharged through a system of pipes and used for irrigation purposes. Should the water in this reservoir become contaminated by the diffusion of the liquid excreta it is drawn off and run into the same system of pipes.

The soil or fall pipe, which is from six to eight inches in diameter, passes vertically from the closet above into the reservoirs. The "cuvette," or bowl of the closet, is of special construction, resembling the bowl first used by Capt. Liernur in his pneumatic system, the posterior wall, or back of the bowl being straight to correspond with that of the soil pipe into which it is introduced, so that the excreta fall without interruption into the reservoir. The apparatus will not admit of a soil pipe curved or bent in any part of its course, as it is intended that the excreta shall drop directly down the soil pipe into the reservoir, and, therefore, the latter must be placed immediately under the closet. This apparatus is also intended to be used without any water flush whatever, the bowl being cleansed from time to time or when soiled, by an attendant, with water and a mop. It has been found that the first flow of water over the top of the reservoir, which corresponds in volume with the excretal matter passed below, is quite limpid and pure in appearance, but it soon becomes contaminated and acquires a putrid odor, which indicates that the protective power of the bed of water has been exhausted, and when this occurs the reservoir has to be emptied and refilled with water. It can readily be seen that the plan could not be applied to our American system of water-closets; where there is a large flush of water, and where it would be quite impossible to place the reservoir in every instance directly under the closets; each closet would have to be provided with a separate reservoir.

THE SYSTEM OF DEPLANQUE.—This need only be mentioned in a few words. It has been used in some of the towns of France for a number of years, but, like most systems of the kind, has proved a failure. In the place of mechanical separation of the liquids and solids, M. Deplanque proposed to precipitate the organic materials held in suspension or dilution by lime-water, in order that they may fall to the bottom of the fossa which is to contain them until removed. This fossa or pit into which the material drops vertically through the soil pipe is made watertight by cement, and is filled with lime-water. When the dejections drop into the water they displace an equal volume of water, which is carried into the nearest sewer by a pipe provided for the purpose, the solid material and precipitate being deposited on the bottom of the pit to be afterwards carted away.

DR. FORBE'S PATENT PRECIPITATING PROCESS has been highly spoken of by scientific authorities, Dr. Voelcker, Chemist to the Royal Agricultural Society of England, among others, having reported favorably of it. The distinguishing feature of this process is the employment of a material which, while it acts as a disinfectant agent, possesses also highly valuable fertilizing properties. The agent employed is the phosphate of alumina dissolved in hydrochloric acid Acting at once as a powerful disinfectant. and adding to the fertilizing value of the clarified and purified sewage, it adds in like proportion to the value of this as an irrigating field.

THE SYSTEM OF SCHLEH.—As the emanations from privies constitute one of their most objectionable features, Mr. Schleh has proposed an arrangement for the absorption of the gases as rapidly as they are formed. The reservoir is to be of iron lined with asphalt; a "trap" or syphon is fixed to the inferior or outfall end of the soil pipe. as well as at the bowl of the closet, which traps are supposed to prevent the gases from entering the house, and, therefore. they are made to pass through a special tube or pipe to two receptacles, the first containing sulphate of iron or manganese, which absorbs the ammonia and sulphureted hydrogen : the second contains sulphuric acid, which decomposes the remaining gases and sets free carbonic acid, which escapes through a pipe passing up to or above the level of the roof. This system has not been practically applied in any place, its advocate resting his claims only on theoretical grounds.

THE GROUX SYSTEM.—This is one of the so-called dry processes. It consists of a movable vessel in the form of a truncated cone, at the bottom of which is placed some deodorizing or absorbent material ; then a solid cone or plug, somewhat smaller than the inner side of the vessel. is inserted, leaving between the inner surface of the vessel and the plug a space of 3 or 4 inches which is to be filled with the absorbent material : the plug or mould is then withdrawn, leaving a central cavity which receives the fæcal matters. When the vessel is filled it is covered by a close fitting cover, and in the removal the lining of absorbent material becomes mixed with the contents of the vessel. The lining substance or absorbent material may consist of the general debris of a farm house, such as sweepings, fragments of straw or fodder, chaff, tan, saw-dust, &c., mixed with a small quantity of earth, plaster, or pulverized charcoal. This system has been used in England and France and is said to have given good results, but it requires, as all similar appliances do, great care and constant attention, and is only suited to small villages and country houses.

CHAPTER XV.

Taylard's System for Emptying Cesspools and Privy Pits.

ONE of the most valuable improvements recently effected in the practical cleansing of cesspools and privy pits is a portable pneumatic pumping apparatus recently patented by M. Taylard, of Paris, and improved by Messrs. Charles & Babillat, Mechanical Engineers, at St. Denis, which practically overcomes one of the objections to cesspools, viz., the inconvenience and offensiveness incident to the operation of emptying and cleansing them.

The Taylard system, adapted to large cities, consists of a pneumatic steam pump mounted on wheels, and an air tight iron tank of the capacity of from 500 to 800 gallons, also on wheels. When the apparatus is to be used the tank is connected with the air pump by a small flexible tube through which the air is drawn out of the tank. For towns of less than 15,000 or 20,000 inhabitants, a small air pump worked by hand performs a similar service to that of the pneumatic steam pump. In either case the emptying is effected by creating a vacuum